HANDS-ON HISTORY

PROJECTS ABOUT
Ancient Greece

Marian Broida

Marshall Cavendish
Benchmark
New York

To Nathan

Acknowledgments

My gratitude to Jasper Gaunt, Curator of Greek and Roman Art, Carlos Museum, Atlanta, Thomas Palaima, Dickson Centennial Professor of Classics, University of Texas at Austin, and Tobi Ames.

Thanks also to the children and adults who tested activities, particularly to regular craft-testers Cana and Taylor McGhee and Deonte Rivers; and also to Aaron and Hannah Freedman, Noa Hardin, Roei Levi, Myron McGhee, Micah and Naomi Rubin, Stephanie Rubin, Sarah Stein, Thandiwe Tinsley, Melissa and Yael Toporek, and Nadav Yeglin.

Benchmark Books
Marshall Cavendish
99 White Plains Road
Tarrytown, NY 10591-9001
www.marshallcavendish.us

Text Copyright © 2006 by Marshall Cavendish Corporation

Illustrations and map Copyright © 2006 by Marshall Cavendish Corporation

Library of Congress Cataloging-in-Publication Data
Broida, Marian.
Projects about ancient Greece / by Marian Broida.
    p. cm. — (Hands-on history)
Summary: "Includes social studies projects taken from the ancient Greeks"—Provided by publisher.
Includes bibliographical references and index.
ISBN-13: 978-0-7614-2259-4
ISBN-10: 0-7614-2259-5
1. Greece—Civilization—To 146 B.C.—Study and teaching (Elementary)—Activity programs—Juvenile literature. 2. Greece—Social life and customs—To 146 B.C.—Study and teaching (Elementary)—Activity programs—Juvenile literature. I. Title. II. Series.

DF77.B85 2006
938—dc22
    2006002805

Title page: A view of the Parthenon, part of the Acropolis in Athens, Greece.
Maps by XNR Productions
Illustrations by Rodica Prato
Photo Research by Joan Meisel

Photo credits: *Art Resource*, NY: 1, *Scala*; 8, Erich Lessing; 42, HIP; *Corbis*: 4, 15, *Bettmann*; 6, Gail Mooney; 18, Araldo de Luca; 35, Werner Forman; *North Wind Picture Archives*: 22, 28, 40; *The Bridgeman Art Library*: 16, *Pushkin Museum*, Moscow, Russia; 24, *Agora Museum*, Athens, Greece.

Printed in China

1 3 5 6 4 2

Contents

An ancient stadium. The first Olympic Games were held at Olympia around 777 BCE.

1
Introduction

For thousands of years, people have lived on the islands and mainland of Greece, raising sheep and goats, growing grapes and olives, and sailing the sea to fish or trade. These creative people invented **democracy**, started the Olympic Games, built beautiful temples, and wrote poems and plays people still read today. For more than two thousand years Greek scientists, writers, artists, and thinkers have inspired people around the world.

In this book you will be visiting ancient Greece in different times and places. You will tour a palace in Crete, make a pottery cup in Corinth, attend a festival in Athens, and paint a shield in Sparta. You will practice two kinds of ancient Greek writing, play "knucklebones," host a dessert party, and more.

Everything in this book happened more than two thousand years ago, before the year 1. When you read 500 BCE, think "five hundred years before the year 1." Some people say 500 BC, which means the same thing. This book uses "BCE."

Enjoy your journey!

The Minoan palace at Knossos in Crete once featured a central courtyard, a throne room, banquet halls, and bathrooms with indoor plumbing.

2

Greece before the Classical Period

In 2000 BCE, a peaceful people called the Minoans (min-OH-uns) lived on the island of Crete and traded with other lands. They spoke their own language (not Greek) and invented their own way of writing. Their kings lived in palaces. The most famous palace, at Knossos, was built like a maze.

Around 1600 BCE, a different group of people called the Myceneans (my-suh-NEE-uns) began building fortlike palaces on the Greek mainland and islands. They took over Crete, too. They changed Minoan writing into **Linear B** in order to write their own language, Greek. They sailed the seas to trade and to fight. They made beautiful pottery and buildings.

All the Greek palaces were destroyed in 1200 BCE—no one is sure exactly why. After that, the Greeks forgot how to do many things, such as writing. Over time, they began doing these things in new ways. Sometime between 800 BCE and 700 BCE, they learned to write again, using an alphabet, and began writing down poems. They created new ways to decorate pottery, held the first Olympic Games, and established **colonies** in other lands. Artists, musicians, poets, builders, and thinkers kept finding new and better ways of doing things. By 500 BCE, the Greeks had developed a great civilization.

Minoan Bull-dancer Painting

The year is 1500 BCE. You are visiting Crete with your father, king of a nearby land. A nobleman is showing you to your rooms. You pass a wall painted with an amazing scene: young men and women somersaulting over a live bull. They are taking turns grabbing the bull's horns and leaping over its back.

"I'll ask the king if you can try that," your father says.

Your heart begins to pound. Then he grins, and you know it was just a joke.

Bull-dancing was a test of grace and bravery for both men and women athletes.

You will need:

- 12 by 8 inch piece of white poster board
- ruler
- pencil
- ten or more strips of gift wrap in different patterns, each about 1 inch wide by 5 to 6 inches long
- scissors
- glue stick
- scrap paper
- thin black pen or marker
- colored markers
- blue crayon (optional)
- one-hole punch or large nail
- yarn or string, 12 inches long

1. Lay the ruler on the poster board, along one edge. Draw a pencil line alongside the ruler. Repeat along the other edges.

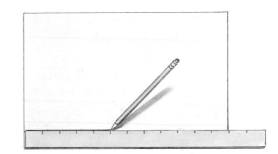

2. Stack several strips of gift wrap, pattern side up. Cut the strips into lengths about 1 ½ inches long. Leave them stacked, if possible. Repeat with the other strips.

3. Trim the gift wrap pieces so they are rounded at one end. Hint: leave them stacked and cut off two corners on one short side.

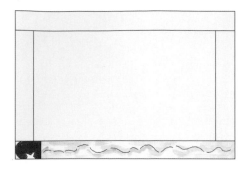

4. Spread glue along one long edge of the poster board, inside your pencil line. Lay a piece of gift wrap in the left corner, with the curve pointing left. Lay another piece with a different pattern next to it, overlapping it a little. Overlap by placing the new piece on top. This piece should also point left. Repeat on the other borders. On the short sides the curves will point up.

5. Copy the picture of the bull and dancers from page 8 on paper. Then draw light pencil lines on the poster board and inside the frame to show where each figure will go. Hint: to make sure you have room, draw the people on the ends before starting the bull.

6. Darken your pencil lines with pen. Color the bull and people with markers. Try blue crayon for the background, or leave it white.

7. To attach the hanger, make a dot 4 inches from each end of the upper border. Use the hole punch or nail to punch holes in the dots. (If you use the nail, get adult help.) Thread the cord into each hole and tie the end with a double knot or square knot.

MACEDONIA

Mt. Olympus

Aegean Sea

Athens

Corinth

PELOPONNESUS

Pylos Sparta

LACONIA

Ionia Sea

CRETE Knossos

Ancient Greeks settled in lands around the Aegean Sea, including its islands.
This map shows places mentioned in this book.

Mycenaean Writing (Linear B)

It is 1290 BCE. Your uncle works in a palace in the city of Pylos, keeping track of all the things needed for big feasts. He uses something called writing. He writes on pieces of clay with a **stylus**.

"Very few people know about writing," he says. "Let me show you how I make a list. First, I draw a picture of the kind of thing I'm counting, like cups or jars. Then, I write the number." He shows you the little lines and circles he uses to write numbers.

You are amazed. You never heard of writing before. It seems almost like magic, not having to remember everything in your head.

You will need:

- paper
- pen or pencil

1. Study the examples on page 14. See if you can figure out the system the Mycenaeans used for writing numbers. If you have trouble, see the hints on that page.

2. Try making a list of these things in Linear B. The answers are at the bottom of page 14.

6 jars
14 horses
28 men
359 women

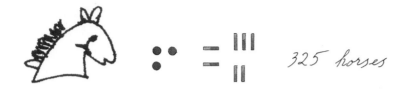

325 horses

1 cup

1256 jars

1 man

2 women

3. Now make a list of everything in your bedroom, your desk, or your kitchen. Invent a symbol for each kind of thing, like *toy* or *book* or *cup*. Count or guess how many books or pens or cups you have. Then, after each symbol, write the number using Linear B.

Hints: Look at how the Myceneans wrote "325 horses." Which part stands for horses? (It's the picture of the horse.) Which part stands for 325? (Everything else!) Think of 325 as three hundreds, two tens, and five ones. Which symbol stands for 100? (What do you see three of?) Which stands for ten? (What do you see two of?) Which stands for one?

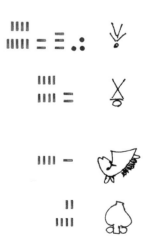

14

According to legend, a small group of Greek warriors hid inside a wooden horse. After entering Troy, the warriors opened the city gates for the rest of the Greek army.

Epic Poem

The year is 740 BCE. It is dark and stuffy behind the wall hanging. You are supposed to be in bed, not hiding in the banquet hall with your brother, waiting to hear an exciting new poem that tells the story about the **Trojan War**.

Just then, the poet begins playing his **lyre**. The sound is so near, it makes you jump.

"Are you sure he can't see us?" you whisper.

"I heard he's blind," your brother whispers back. "Now hush! He's starting the poem!"

The two most famous Greek poems are *The Iliad* and *The Odyssey*. *The Iliad* is about the hero Odysseus and the Trojan War. For thousands of years, Greeks believed these poems were written by a blind poet named Homer, but this might just be a story.

1. Practice reading the poem aloud. If it's not too long, think about memorizing it.

2. Gather the audience. Pass out the refreshments.

3. Begin by playing a little on your musical instrument.

4. Read or recite the poem, speaking slowly and clearly. Show the characters' feelings in your voice. Play a few chords between verses.

5. If you like, wear ancient Greek clothing (see pages 29 and 30).

Black-figure pottery was first made in Corinth. Later, Athenians began making it too. Their work often featured athletes. These two men are boxing.

Black-figure pottery

It is the year 690 BCE. Your father is a painter of clay jars and cups in Corinth. You love watching him work. First, he draws a lion on the clay jar. Then, he fills in the drawing with black paint to make it look like a shadow. After it dries, he cuts through the paint with a sharp tool, drawing the lion's eye and other details. No other artist does this last step. Your father invented it.

One day you see a jar painted by another man. The dogs painted on the jar have eyes cut through the paint.

"Father, someone stole your idea!" you say.

Your father shakes his head. "Such ideas come from the gods," he says. "They are meant to be shared."

You will need:

- newspaper or plastic to protect table
- 8-ounce plastic yogurt container, clean and dry
- one package red-, yellow-, or terra-cotta colored Model Magic
- three 12-inch pipe cleaners
- scissors
- paper
- black permanent marker
- alcohol wipe to clean hands

1. Spread the plastic or newspaper on the table.

2. Cover the outside of the yogurt container (except the bottom) with a thin layer of Model Magic. Hint: (Make clay pancakes and stick them to the cup, then fill in the gaps.) If you have enough clay, cover the inside, too. Make sure to leave enough clay for the handles.

3. Cut a pipe cleaner in half.

4. Fold another pipe cleaner in half. Use one of the cut halves to wrap around and around the folded pipe cleaner. Cover it with Model Magic and roll it into a sausage. Curve it so it looks like one side of a heart. Attach it near the top and bottom of the cup.

5. Repeat steps 3 and 4 to make a handle for the other side.

6. With the marker, design a border on paper. A popular Greek border is called a key pattern (see picture).

7. If you like, use the marker to draw outlines of people or animals. Then fill them in completely with black marker.

key pattern

8. After the cup has dried for at least 15 minutes, copy your border on the cup near the top or bottom of the cup (or both). Add filled–in black pictures if you like.

9. Let the cup dry for twenty-four hours. It's okay if the clay cracks—that will only make it look older. Use the cup as a decoration, not for food or drink.

Most of the plays written during the Classical period were intended for performance in the Theater of Dionysos in Athens. A ticket cost two *obals*, more than a laborer earned in one day.

3

Classical Period

In the years from 500 BCE to 323 BCE, Greeks created democracy and great works of art: plays, buildings, and statues. Many Greeks lived in **city-states**, such as Athens and Sparta.

Athens was the most famous. Beautiful temples built to honor Athena, the city's special goddess, stood on a hill called the Acropolis (ah-CRAH-poe-liss). For wealthy men Athens was a place to attend theater and dinner parties, and to take part in politics. But for women, slaves, and foreigners, Athens was a place of hard work and few rights, such as the right to vote.

Athens' main rival was Sparta. From childhood, Spartan men trained to be tough soldiers in order to keep control over their many slaves. During the Peloponnesian (peh-loe-poe-NEE-shun) War, Athens and Sparta fought each other.

In 336 BCE, Alexander the Great became the young king of **Macedonia** (mah-suh-DOE-nee-ya). His armies spread Greek culture to Persia, Egypt, and India. The Classical period ended with his death in 323 BCE.

Athenian Ostrakon

You and your parents are foreigners living in Athens in 472 BCE. You are helping them sell pottery in the market. You overhear two **citizens** talking about whether to vote to **ostracize**, or banish, someone. One man says, "I hope we ostracize Themistokles (the-MISS-toe-kleez) today. He's too powerful—he might take over Athens and end our democracy!"

"If enough citizens write his name on an **ostrakon**, he'll be kicked out of Athens for ten years," says the other man.

"Will you vote to ostracize him?" you ask your mother.

"I can't vote," she says. "Only citizens can vote. Neither foreigners nor women can be citizens, and I'm both."

An ostrakon, a piece of clay with a name scratched onto it. The name on this one is Themistokles, an Athenian statesman.

1. Paint a thin coat of paint on one side of the flower-pot or saucer. Let it dry. (This may take 30 minutes or more.)

2. Meanwhile, think of someone famous you think should leave the country for ten years. Write the name in English on scrap paper.

3. Still using scrap pa-per, write the same name using the Greek alphabet (see pages 26 and 27). First, think about how the name sounds. Find Greek letters standing for those sounds. Then read the spelling tips that follow.

4. When the paint is dry, scratch the name in the paint with the nail, using Greek letters.

The Greek Alphabet

The Greek alphabet is older than the one we use for English. The word *alphabet* comes from the names of the first two letters: alpha and beta. Some letters look like letters in the English alphabet but stand for different sounds, such as *P* (which sounds like our letter *R*) and *Y* (which sounds like "oo").

The Greek letter X stands for a sound we don't usually use in English.

This chart has only capital letters. The Greeks did not begin using small letters until centuries later.

Spelling tips:

For *c*, use Kappa (**K**) or Sigma (**Σ**), depending on whether you pronounce the *c* like *k* or *s*.

For *j*, use Iota (**I**).

For *v*, use Phi (**Φ**).

For *w*, use Omicron Upsilon (**OY**)

For long *i* as in *I* or *wide*, use Alpha Iota (**AI**)

Greek Letter	Name of Letter	Sounds Like Letter
A	Alpha	a, as in father
B	Beta	b, as in boy
Γ	Gamma	g, as in girl
Δ	Delta	d, as in dog
E	Epsilon	e, as in bed
Z	Zeta	z, as in zoo
H	Eta	ey, as in they, or a as in made
Θ	Theta	th, as in thing
I	Iota	i, as in big, or ee, as in feet
K	Kappa	k, as in king, or c, as in come
Λ	Lambda	l, as in lion
M	Mu	m, as in mouse
N	Nu	n, as in needle
Ξ	Xi ("ksee")	x, as in next
O	Omicron	o, as in not
Π	Pi	p, as in pig
P	Rho	r, as in road
Σ	Sigma	s, as in sit
T	Tau	t, as in toad
Y	Upsilon	oo, as in book, or u as in universe
Φ	Phi	f, as in friend, or ph, as in phone
X	Chi	ch, as in ache, Bach
Ψ	Psi	ps, as in hops
Ω	Omega	o, as in bone

Greek Clothing

It is the yearly birthday festival of Athena—a week of sports and music contests in honor of the goddess. The year is 440 BCE. For nine months, a few specially chosen women and girls have been weaving the goddess a new gown. Today is the most important event of the festival. There will be a grand march to the Acropolis, where the gown will be put on a statue of Athena. Rich and poor, citizen and foreigner, adult and child—nearly everyone in Athens will take part.

You smooth the wool of your brand-new **chiton** (KIE-tun). Your sister wove it and gave it to you just in time for the festival. It does not have pictures of heroes on it, like Athena's gown. But Athena, after all, is a goddess. You are only human—and you want to look your best.

Women wore various forms of the chiton in the fifth century BCE.

1. Measure and cut the fabric. The width is the distance from elbow to elbow when the arms are spread wide, multiplied by two. For girls, the length is the distance from shoulder to ground, plus 18 inches. For boys, the length is the distance from the shoulder to knee, plus 18 inches.

2. Lay the fabric on the ground. Keep track of which side is the length and which side is the width! Fold down the top 18 inches of the length.

←——— Key pattern

3. Optional: Use permanent markers to draw a pattern, such as the key design shown above on this page, along the border you just folded down. Hint: Lay scrap paper underneath the fabric before you draw on it so the ink doesn't leak through. Draw another border along the bottom.

4. Wrap the fabric around you, leaving the top part folded down in front and back. One side will be open. Have a helper pin the fabric at each shoulder.

5. Tie the belt around your waist. You can let the folded part of the fabric drape over the belt or tuck it in if it is long enough. Boys can wear two belts—one around the hips and one around the waist.

6. Arrange the folds evenly. Pull a bit of fabric up over the belt or belts.

Spartan Shield

You are visiting your aunt and uncle in the year 390 BCE. Their son, your cousin, just died fighting Athenians.

"He fought bravely, as he trained to do from childhood," your aunt says. "That is what matters."

"His shield was too heavy," says your uncle. "Lately, some of the Athenians have been using straw shields instead of wooden ones. Their soldiers can move much faster."

"We Spartans do not like change," says your aunt.

You will need:

- large round saucer of flexible plastic, about 16 inches in diameter with a rim at least 1 inch wide, meant to go under a planter or flowerpot
- poster board or thicker cardboard, slightly larger than the saucer
- pencil
- scissors
- duct tape
- one-hole punch
- rope or clothesline, its length about 2 ½ times the diameter of plant saucer
- partial roll of sticky-backed shelf paper, enough to cover the saucer plus 1 to 2 inches
- acrylic paints
- paintbrushes
- an adult helper

1. Trace around the saucer onto the cardboard with the pencil. Cut along your lines. Lay the cutout cardboard inside the saucer. Trim if necessary.

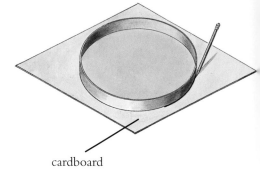

cardboard

2. Fasten in place with five to six small pieces of duct tape.

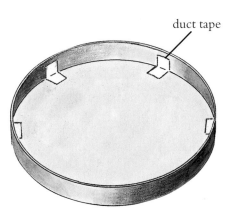

duct tape

3. Punch a hole in the rim of the saucer. Enlarge it by punching two to three more overlapping holes.

4. Punch one more hole directly opposite the first, all the way around on the other side of the shield.

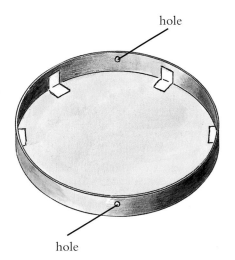

hole

hole

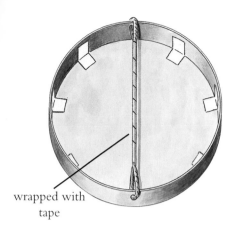

wrapped with tape

5. Thread the rope through both holes. Overlap the loose ends in the middle. Hold them together. Ask your helper to wrap duct tape around and around the overlapped ends. (Hint: unroll the tape right onto the rope.) Leave about 3 inches unwrapped on each end of the rope.

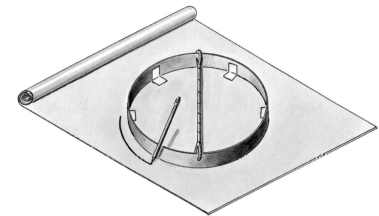

6. Unroll about 18 inches of shelf paper (1 to 2 inches wider than diameter of shield), sticky side up. Lay the shield facedown on top.

7. With a pencil, trace around the shield onto the sticky side of the paper, $\frac{1}{2}$ to 1 inch away from the edge of the shield.

8. Cut the paper along your pencil line. Fold down the edges onto the rim of the shield.

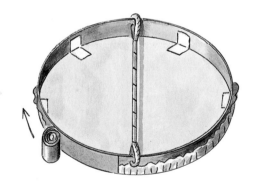

9. Hold the shield steady while your helper unrolls duct tape neatly all around the rim of the shield, hiding the edge of the shelf paper. When you come to a spot where the rope comes out, cut the tape. Start taping again past the rope.

10. Turn the shield faceup, with the rope running up and down in back. Paint a decoration on the front. The Spartans often used the Greek letter Lambda (see pages 26 and 27), which stood for Laconia (la-COE-nee-ya), the area around Sparta.

Knucklebones

It is 356 BCE. All the men and boys in your family have gone to the Olympics to watch the races and other sports. Since you're a girl, you have to stay behind. Wealthy girls and women hardly ever leave their houses, where they spend much of their time cooking and weaving.

"Why can't we go to the Olympics?" you ask your mother.

"Married women aren't allowed at the Olympics," your mother answers. "Unmarried girls are, but I would never let you go without me."

"Cheer up," your sister says. "Let's stop weaving and play knucklebones. We can crown the winner with a wreath, just like they do at the Olympics."

You will need:

- Model Magic, 1 ounce or more ($\frac{1}{2}$ ounce will make two or three knucklebones)

---

1. Look at the drawings of knucklebones on page 36.

2. Form a ball of Model Magic about the size of a quarter. Flatten each side on the table to make a small block.

3. Pinch it several times in different places. Try giving it a "waist," or pressing one end in, and pushing another end out. No two knucklebones were exactly alike.

4. Make at least five. Let them dry (usually an hour or less).

5. Play knucklebones!

Ancient Greek boys and girls played games with dried anklebones of sheep or goats, called knucklebones in English. Some games were like marbles and others were like jacks.

Girls' Play: Pentelithoi

Here is one game, called *pentelithoi* which is Greek for "five stones." The game is a lot like the modern game of jacks. This game was popular with women and girls.

1. Take turns with a friend.

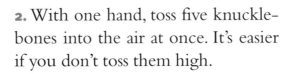

2. With one hand, toss five knuckle-bones into the air at once. It's easier if you don't toss them high.

3. Catch as many as you can on the back of your throwing hand. This takes practice. It helps to bend your fingers back and spread them out.

4. If all the knucklebones fall to the ground, your turn is over. If you catch them all, you win.

5. If you catch one to four bones, leave them on the back of your hand while you try to pick up the ones that fell. If you can pick them all up and not drop any, take another turn.

Boys' Play: Knucklebones

Here is another game, more popular with boys.

1. Draw a circle about two feet across. You can use chalk on a sidewalk or a marker on a piece of poster board.

2. Gather one to two other friends to play.

3. Set two or more knucklebones inside the circle, keeping one out for each player.

4. Take turns trying to knock knucklebones out of the circle by throwing your knucklebone at them. Pick up your knucklebone after each throw. If you knock one out, keep it till the end of the game and take another turn.

5. The game ends when all the knucklebones have been knocked out. The winner is the one with the most knucklebones at the end.

Dessert Party (Symposium)

"You! Slave! Bring in the dessert tables!" your master calls from his couch. It is the year 333 BCE. Your master is hosting a party called a **symposium**. Three guests, all men, lie on other couches around the room: two poets and a sculptor.

You carry in a small table for each guest. Each table is loaded with small dishes of goodies. As you serve the sculptor, a dish of pastry crashes to the floor.

"Those *staititai* (STY-tee-tie)," the sculptor says. "They always fall sticky-side down."

You will need:

- tablecloth or tarp
- four large plastic bags
- four cushions or pillows
- four place mats
- four plates and napkins. No silverware: ancient Greeks ate with their hands
- four cups filled with grape juice
- ancient Greek dessert foods, such as olives, hard-boiled eggs, almonds or walnuts, apples or grapes, raisins or dried figs

1. Spread the cloth on the floor or the ground. Put the pillows into the plastic bags and place them around the cloth. Invite guests to lie around the cloth with pillows under their sides.

2. Bring each guest a place mat. On it, arrange a cup of juice, a napkin, and a plate loaded with food. The guests should prop themselves up on their elbow and eat with their other hand. They should talk about important subjects, perhaps something in the news.

3. If you like, entertain the guests by singing, dancing, juggling, or reciting poetry.

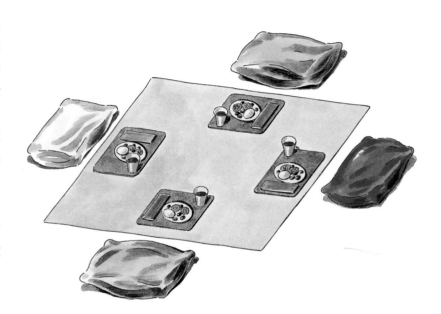

Quick Recipe for *Staititai*

Here's a quick version of *staititai* you might want to try: Spread shortbread cookies with honey and ricotta cheese, then sprinkle with toasted sesame seeds. One tablespoon each of honey, cheese, and seeds is enough for 6 cookies.

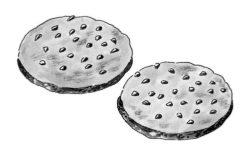

Alexander the Great's army entered Egypt in 332 BCE. He was welcomed as a hero, and founded the city of Alexandria in Egypt.

4
Hellenistic Period

After Alexander the Great died in 323 BCE, his generals divided the lands he had conquered into three parts: Greece (including Macedonia), Egypt, and the land from Syria all the way to India's border. His generals ruled these lands as kings, and their relatives ruled after them. This period is called Hellenistic, because Hellas is the Greek name for Greece.

Greek customs mixed with local customs, especially in the cities. Wealthier people began wearing Greek-style clothes, building Greek-style buildings, playing Greek sports, and speaking Greek. The Greeks learned new customs, too. For example, in Egypt, people worshipped their kings and queens as gods. This custom spread to Athens in Hellenistic times.

Meanwhile, the city of Rome was building its own empire. As Rome rose in power, Greece became weaker. In 146 BCE, the Roman Empire took over Greece. But the Greek way of life did not die out. The Romans admired the Greeks and spread their ideas everywhere they ruled.

Herakles Knot

The year is 215 BCE. Your father, a wealthy man, often travels across the sea to trade. Today he returned with a beautiful gold head decoration for your mother and a bracelet for you.

"Look," he says. "These were made in Egypt. They both have the same design in the middle. It's called a **Herakles** (HER-uh-kleez) knot, named after the hero. It's supposed to be able to heal wounds and protect you from evil." He gives both of you the jewelry. Your mother arranges the head decoration so the knot appears right over her eyes. You put the heavy bracelet on your upper arm.

"Don't wear that in the street," your mother tells you. "It's too valuable. It might get stolen."

"Can't the Herakles knot protect against theft?" you ask.

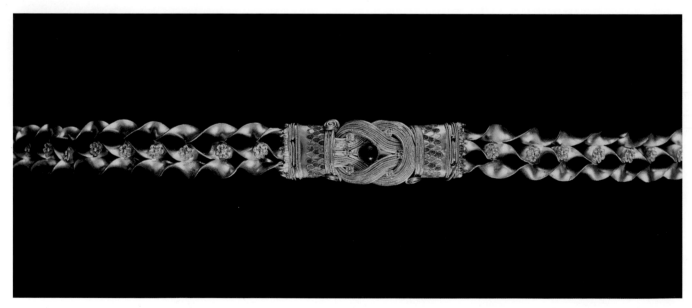

A Herakles knot decorates the center of this elegant headband made in the third century BCE.

You will need:

- twelve-inch gold pipe cleaners: five for an armband, six for a head decoration
- a helper for the last step
- scissors (needed for armband only)

1. Hold two pipe cleaners together, side by side. Match up their ends. Bend them into a narrow U. Lay it down. Repeat with two more pipe cleaners, so that you have two narrow U shapes.

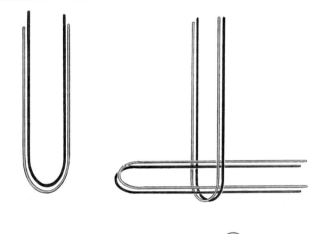

2. Hold one U with its legs pointing up. Place the other U inside the first, so that it is flat with its legs pointing toward you. Push it about halfway through the first U.

3. Gently bend the legs of the first (upright) U and tuck them through the curve of the other U (the one lying flat). This is the hardest step.

4. Pull all four sets of legs gently until the legs are about the same length on each side. Don't pull all the way! It should look like an H with a hollow circle or oval in the middle. This is a Herakles knot.

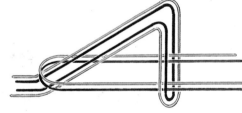

inner legs

5. To turn your Herakles knot into a piece of jewelry, keep the pipe cleaners as flat and even as possible.

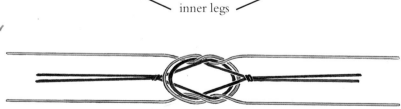

6. On one end of the middle circle, find the two inner legs. Twist the inner legs around each other once or twice, near the knot. The end of the legs should lie straight and flat. Repeat on the other side.

7. With one outer leg, fold the tip over itself toward the outside. Fold it over and over itself to make a flat spiral pointing away from the knot. See the picture.

8. Repeat step 7 with the other three outer legs. Make sure the knot and legs lie flat.

9. Find the straight ends of the pipe cleaner on one side of the knot. Twist the tips together two or three times to form a circle. Repeat on the other side with the other two straight ends. Now do either step 10 or step 11.

10. To make a head ornament, attach a pipe cleaner to each of the two side circles. Put it on your head with the design in front. Have a helper twist the two ends together in back.

11. To make an armband, wrap the knot gently around your upper arm. Have a helper poke the last pipe cleaner through each of the side circles. Twist the ends of this pipe cleaner together to get a good fit. If this pipe cleaner is much too long, trim the ends with scissors.

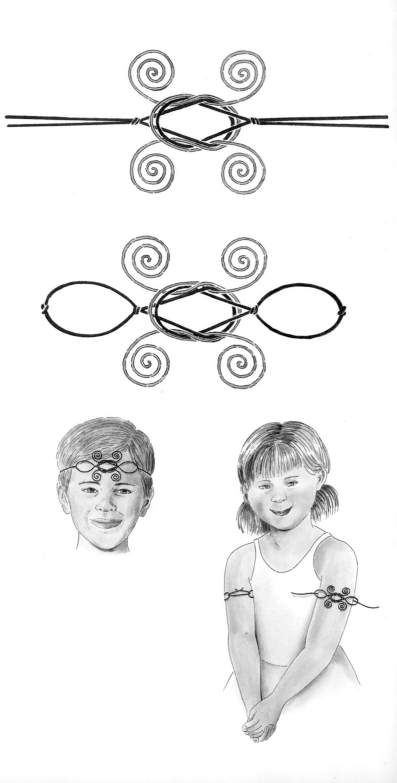

Glossary

alphabet: A series of letters, usually fewer than forty that stand for individual vowels or consonants. The earliest writing systems, like Linear B, did not use alphabets.

BCE (or BC): Written after a date, it means the number of years before the year 1.

chiton: A piece of clothing made of cloth fastened at both shoulders, worn by ancient Greek men and women. Women's chitons were longer than the men's.

citizens: Residents of a city or country who have rights and responsibilities.

city-state: An independent city that governs the land and people around it.

colony: A group of people who leave their own country and settle in another distant land.

democracy: A kind of government in which citizens have political power and can vote.

epic: A long poem that tells the story of a hero. *The Iliad* and *The Odyssey* are famous Greek epic poems.

Herakles: Another way to say Hercules, a famous Greek hero.

Linear B: A system of writing used by Mycenaeans in ancient Greece 3200 years ago, mostly for making lists. Five hundred years later, Greeks developed their alphabet.

lyre: Musical instrument with strings. Poets played lyres while they recited their poems.

Macedonia: A region in northern Greece with its own king.

ostracize: In ancient Athens, to force a statesman out of the city, usually for ten years.

ostrakon: Piece of broken pottery used in ancient Greek democracy. Citizens voted to **ostracize**, or banish, politicians they didn't like by writing their names on an ostrakon.

staititai **(plural):** A kind of pastry spread with honey, sesame seeds, and cheese.

stylus: A small, thin stick or reed with a bladelike point, used to write in clay.

symposium: An after-dinner party for men only, with entertainment, dessert, and wine.

Trojan War: A war in which the Greeks attacked the city of Troy in the country now called Turkey. The Trojan War is described in the ancient Greek poem *The Iliad*.

Metric Conversion Chart

You can use the chart below to convert from U. S. measurements to the metric system.

Weight
1 ounce = 28 grams
½ pound (8 ounces) = 227 grams
1 pound = .45 kilogram
2.2 pounds = 1 kilogram

Liquid volume
1 teaspoon = 5 milliliters
1 tablespoon = 15 milliliters
1 fluid ounce = 30 milliliters
1 cup = 240 milliliters (.24 liter)
1 pint = 480 milliliters (.48 liter)
1 quart = .95 liter

Length
¼ inch = .6 centimeter
½ inch = 1.25 centimeters
1 inch = 2.5 centimeters

Temperature
100°F = 40°C
110°F = 45°C
350°F = 180°C
375°F = 190°C
400°F = 200°C
425°F = 220°C
450°F = 235°C

About the Author

Marion Broida has a special interest in hands-on history for children. Growing up near George Washington's home in Mount Vernon, Virginia, Ms. Broida spent much of her childhood pretending she lived in colonial America. She has written eight other titles in the Hands-On History series. In addition to children's activity books, she writes books for adults on health care topics and occasionally works as a nurse. Ms. Broida lives in Decatur, Georgia.

Find Out More

Books

Chrisp, Peter. *Alexander the Great: The Legend of a Warrior King*. New York: Dorling Kindersley, 2000.

Connolly, Peter, and Hazel Dodge. *The Ancient City: Life in Classical Athens and Rome*. New York: Oxford University Press, 2000.

Hodge, Susie. *Ancient Greek Art*. Des Plaines, IL: Heinemann Interactive Library, 1998.

Nardo, Don. *Ancient Greece*. San Diego: Blackbirch Press, 2004.

Pearson, Anne. Eyewitness Books. *Ancient Greece*. New York: Knopf Books for Young Readers, 1992.

Ross, Steward. Ancient Greece. *Daily Life*. Lincolnwood, IL: Peter Bedrick Books, 1999.

Web Sites

The Ancient Olympics
http://www.perseus.tufts.edu/Olympics/index.html

Costume in Ancient Greece
http://www.annaswebart.com/culture/costhistory/ancient/

Odyssey Online: Greece
http://carlos.emory.edu/ODYSSEY/GREECE/homepg.html

Index

Page numbers in **boldface** are illustrations.

map, 12

Alexander the Great, 23, **40**, 41
architecture, **6**, 7, 23
art, **8**, 9–11
Athens, **12**, **22**, 23, 24, 28, 31
athletics, 7, 8, **8**, **18**, 28, 34

civilization, 5, 7, 23, 41
Classical Period, 7, 23
clothes and jewelry, **28**, 28–30, 42, **42**
Corinth, **12**, **18**, 19
Crete, **6**, 7, 8–10, **9**, **12**, **13**

education, 31
Egypt, **40**, 41, 42, **42**

food, 38, 39
foreigners, 23, 24, 28

games, 34–37, **35**, **36**, **37**.
    See also athletics
gods and goddesses, 19, 23, 28, 41

government, 5, 23, 24, **24**

Hellenistic period, 41
Herakles knot, **42**, 43–44
Homer, 16, **16**
language, 7, 41. *See also* writing

Macedonia, **12**, 23, 41
Minoans, **6**, 7
musical instruments, 16
Myceneans, 7, 13–14

parties, **16**, 16–17, 38–39, **39**
poems, 16–17
pottery, 7, **18**, 19–21
projects
    bull-dancer art, 9–11
    carving ostrakon, 25
    chiton (outfit), 29–30, **30**
    entertaining guests
        with poem, 17
    Herakles knot, 43–44, **43–44**
    knucklebones, 34, **36**,
        36–37, **37**
    recipe, 39
    symposium, 38–39
    pottery, 19–21

Spartan shield, 32–33, **33**
writing in Linear B, 13–14, **14**

slavery, 23, 38
Sparta, 23, 31–33
Syria, 41

theater, **22**, 23

war, **15**, 16, 23, 31
women, 23, 24, **28**, 34, 36
writing
    alphabet, 26–27
    numbers, 13–14, **14**, 36

48